AS ONE

BUNKER OR BASECAMP?

SUSAN HARPER BARNETT

outskirtspress
DENVER, COLORADO

Scripture quotations marked NKJ are taken from the New King James Version, copyright 1982 by Thomas Nelson, Inc. Used by permission. All rights reserved. Scripture quotations marked CJB are taken from the Complete Jewish Bible, copyright 1998 by David H. Stern. Published by Jewish New Testament Publications, Inc. www.messianicjewish.net/jntp. Distributed by Messianic Jewish Resources Int'l. www.messianicjewish.net. All rights reserved. AENT refers to the Aramic English New Testament. Scripture taken from the Aramaic English New Testament. Copyright 2008. Used by permission of Netzari Press.

The opinions expressed in this manuscript are solely the opinions of the author and do not represent the opinions or thoughts of the publisher. The author has represented and warranted full ownership and/or legal right to publish all the materials in this book.

As One
Bunker or Basecamp?
All Rights Reserved.
Copyright © 2016 Susan Harper Barnett
v3.0

Cover Photo © 2016 thinkstockphotos.com. All rights reserved - used with permission.

This book may not be reproduced, transmitted, or stored in whole or in part by any means, including graphic, electronic, or mechanical without the express written consent of the publisher except in the case of brief quotations embodied in critical articles and reviews.

Outskirts Press, Inc.
http://www.outskirtspress.com

ISBN: 978-1-4787-6930-9

Outskirts Press and the "OP" logo are trademarks belonging to Outskirts Press, Inc.

PRINTED IN THE UNITED STATES OF AMERICA

# FOREWORD

This book by Susan will open your eyes to some of the layers beneath the discussion of the Apostolic Church. I have read and heard many speak about the fivefold ministry. What normally comes to me when I read what they have written, or hear what they have said, is that they really do not understand what fivefold ministry is about. You will be happy to know that I did not feel that way with this book.

I have spent time with Susan and her husband, Mike Barnett, in their home in Denham Springs, Louisiana. They have developed a wonderful Christian community in their region that endeavors to bring to life the wine skin of the fivefold ministry. I was pleased while there to interact with people who are living as apostles, prophets, teachers, evangelists, and pastors.

Fivefold ministry is not a new thing at all. In fact, many of the ministers and leaders who are in the church today are actually walking as one of the five gifts to the church, but because they do not understand what it is that they are living, they become frustrated and unfulfilled.

From my perspective, the reason that we want to be comfortable with fivefold ministry is so that the church understands the gift that they are receiving into their midst, but more importantly, so that they position themselves to receive the full measure of the anointing and gift that this ministry can release. If you are trying to receive someone as a pastor when that person is a prophet, do not be surprised when they fail to minister to you in the way that you desire.

I have had many people want to receive me as a pastor or evangelist. I find this uncomfortable. When I encounter these people I know that they have preconceived notions of what it is I am to do in their midst. I have given up trying to live by other people's expectations. I try to live as I am designed, which means educating the church to the fivefold ministry.

Many people, when talking about the fivefold, will quickly say that they are not into titles, meaning that it is somehow a matter of pride to call oneself an apostle or prophet. But these same people have no problem calling themselves pastors or evangelists.

Receiving someone as a prophet or apostle or teacher is not about adding a title to a name, but rather about recognizing the gift that God has sent to you. If someone sends you a box of chocolates for your birthday and you go around saying you got a dozen flowers you are causing unnecessary confusion. Moreover, if I am a prophet calling myself a pastor it means that I am not comfortable in my own ministry skin and therefore the church that I serve will be frustrated, as will I. I know of an older prophet in Canada who suffers from mental illness because the church could not understand his gifting as prophet. He now lives in a basement apartment, not willing to see anyone. People like this broke the ground for a generation to rise up into their proper apostolic identities.

This book will help you. It will inform you. It will give you a language to be able to start the discussion of the fivefold in your own communities. I pray that you will be enlightened with revelation as you embark on your own journey of discovery.

Darren Wesley Canning
Revivalist Prophet and Teacher

PREFACE

We recently had an interesting experience with our daughter. She had taken her car in for an oil change and tire rotation. I dropped her off when it was ready to be picked up. When I was only a short distance down the road, I got a phone call from her. Her back left tire had fallen off her car while she was driving and had rolled out into the other side of the highway. Fortunately, she was fine and no other vehicles were involved in this mishap.

I later came to realize what an accurate reflection of the church this was. Our daughter was driving what should have been a fully functioning vehicle, headed in a predetermined direction, having no reason not to arrive successfully at its destination. Suddenly, a part of that vehicle took off in another direction of its own volition. That event served to disrupt not only the proper function and operation of the vehicle but successfully disrupted its successful arrival at its predetermined destination.

Why did this happen? It happened because when the tires

were put back on the vehicle, they were not properly assembled. A small, yet significant part was left off. This improper assembly prevented the tires from moving as one in one direction serving their purpose to take that vehicle and our daughter successfully to the predetermined destination.

˙ It is possible for the church to function properly. It is possible for the church to operate as it is intended to operate. It is possible for the church to successfully arrive at its predetermined destination. It is possible for the church to move AS ONE. This is only possible, however, if the church is properly assembled. This book contains a proposal concerning what this assembly might look like.

# TABLE OF CONTENTS

Foreword i
Preface v
Introduction 1
Chapter One
    Embracing the Full Expression of Christ 9
Chapter Two
    As One 14
Chapter Three
    On Common Ground 21
Chapter Four
    The Apostolic Grace 29
Chapter Five
    The Prophetic Grace 45
Chapter Six
    Take a Breath 54
Chapter Seven
    The Teaching Grace 61

Chapter Eight
    The Evangelistic Grace 70
Chapter Nine
    The Pastoral Grace 80
Chapter Ten
    We Can Do This! 88
Works Cited 91

INTRODUCTION

And He Himself gave some to be apostles, some prophets, some evangelists, and some pastors and teachers for the equipping of the saints for the work of ministry, for the edifying of the body of Christ, till we all come to the unity of the faith and the knowledge of the Son of God, to a perfect man to the measure of the stature of the fullness of Christ. (Ephesians 4:11-13 NKJ)

We have heard much about fivefold ministry, team ministry, and apostolic and prophetic restoration. What does all of this mean? Why are we talking about it? Why does it matter? What does it mean for you as an individual? First, why is this important? Why should you bother continuing to read? These are the first questions I needed answers to before I began this endeavor. The answer I felt the Lord gave me is, "The church has been operating on one cylinder." This seemed an odd answer. What does that have to do with this topic?! It was time for further inquiry.

After my initial panic, I remembered that He must know that I have some understanding of cylinders or He would not have answered in that way. I regrouped and recalled a class in graduate school in which we discussed cylinders. It was a stretch, but I knew if I dug deep He would recall what He wanted me to remember. That would be enough.

Given that my knowledge is very basic, this is what I remembered. First, running on one cylinder is not good unless you are a small machine such as a lawn mower, motorcycle, or weed eater. A large machine, such as a car, truck, or airplane, will not operate efficiently on one cylinder. It will be said to be "running rough." It will vibrate and shake to the point that parts might fall off. In short, it is not stable. It will not operate as intended. That sounds like the church.

Secondly, the cylinder speaks to the power of an engine, not to its strength. Strength refers to contained potential. This depends on other things as well, such as engine size. Power, on the other hand, refers to released potential. At this point, I was really regretting that I had not taken the class more seriously.

In explanation, it is obvious that a body builder has a lot of strength—contained potential. Power or released potential is not seen, however, until he actually exerts his strength in some way, such as by lifting a barbell. What does it mean then that the church has been running on one cylinder given that number of cylinders speaks to power or released potential?

How much strength or contained potential does the church

have? The church has available the unlimited strength of God Almighty! This is the potential—unlimited!!! How much power or released potential does the church display? Simply said, the church of today, in large part, displays only that which is made possible by the function of one cylinder. Now, it was beginning to make sense to me.

The church has access to the unlimited strength of the Creator of all things but she has been operating on just one tiny part. The church is like a champion body builder who lifts a five-pound weight! His strength is being underused—what a waste of potential! The cylinders Christ gave the church are: apostle, prophet, teacher, evangelist, and pastor. Churches, local expressions of organized religion, have, for the most part, operated under the function of just one of these cylinders. There is most often one person in charge of the operation.

This one cylinder in charge of a local church is frequently called "pastor," regardless of what his true gifting is. Over time, it becomes obvious what their true cylinder function or gifting is by the atmosphere that is created in the gatherings they give oversight to. If there is an evangelist calling himself "pastor," the prevailing evidence will be constant outreaches, community activities, and programs. He is a fun guy, all about providing an activity for everyone to be involved in for the purpose of convincing as many people as possible to "join the church." If the "pastor" is really a teacher there will be word, word, word, word, word to the frustration of those who want to do, do, do, do, do. Evidence that one gifted as a pastor, as we know him, is at the helm is seen in an atmosphere in which every effort is made to keep everyone safe, happy, at home, committed to the good of the house and dependent upon the house. If the "pastor" is really a prophet, the house will be filled with goose bumps and experiences but might be lacking in word ministry. Woe to the local expression that is operated solely by an apostle calling himself "pastor," for indeed the people shall feel plowed over by his drive to see order established without explanation. As you have read this, have you been able to identify local gatherings that fit the descriptions?

What we have seen is the operation of one of these cylinders in local gatherings. The one cylinder in operation then becomes the dominant influence in the house. This leads to development of a very distinct atmosphere that primarily expresses that cylinder's function. We see evidence of this in local gatherings or churches that we can identify as missions oriented or outreach oriented. We see this in churches that have the reputation of being a "hospital for the hurting." Other cylinders, such as the prophet or evangelist, might pass through occasionally to leave a deposit. They stir things up and get people excited and involved. They might bring in a sort of power surge. Then they leave and the deposit they brought to the atmosphere fades as the dominant cylinder returns to its function as the only one in full operation. The power surge diminishes again to that of one cylinder.

Christ did not give one expression of Himself for the equipping of believers. Christ gave five expressions of Himself to accomplish this purpose! If we lock all five graces into their proper function, the level of power, or released potential, will rise to the level of available strength, or contained potential. We will witness an incredible manifestation of His power!

My next thought in the process was one of concern about the idea of operating on five cylinders. With five cylinders, an odd number, the same vibrating and shaking still occurs. Things still run rough. What or who would bring completion? Who must be joined to the five in order for things to run smoothly at optimal power? The sixth cylinder is Holy Spirit. When the apostle, prophet, teacher, evangelist, and pastor work together with Holy Spirit, full potential can be released. Maximum strength, or contained potential, can then be released as maximum power or release potential. Suddenly, the body builder is lifting his maximum weight!

Therefore, the first reason this content is worth our time is because . . .

WE DO NOT WANT TO BE RUNNING ON ONE CYLINDER!

Secondly, this discussion is worth our time because we want to be a complete expression of Christ. He was the greatest Teacher ever! The greatest Apostle ever! The greatest Evangelist, Prophet, and Pastor ever! He demonstrated each of these then left all five of these expressions of Himself to us. Therefore, if we want to be a complete expression of Him, as He was of His Father, we must not only believe in the relevance of all five but we must seek to have all five expressions imparted to us. Just like the cylinders, if we receive impartation from only one, that is the only expression we will manifest.

Now, let us consider Ephesians 4:11–13 in reverse. Unity of the faith has not happened yet, therefore, the content of these scriptures must still apply. Saints, which refers to all believers, are to be prepared for something. That something is the work of Ministry, that is, our assignment—which, in short, is to be administrators of His Kingdom on earth. All believers are to be prepared to do this work, not just an elite group of titled people. The preparation of all believers is the responsibility of those to whom Christ gave the assignment. Who was the assignment given to? It was given to the apostle, prophet, teacher, evangelist, and pastor. They are assigned to equip all believers. In order to be fully equipped, all believers must be taught, trained, and activated by each of the five expressions of Himself which Christ gave the church.

These things we conclude:

1. The charge given in Ephesians 4 is still relevant.
2. The assignment was given to the apostle, prophet, teacher, evangelist, and pastor.
3. The assignment was given by Christ.
4. The assignment involves the process of teaching, training, and activating.
5. The assignment is for the benefit of all believers.
6. The purpose of the assignment is that all believers might be enabled to be administrators of the Kingdom of Yahweh on earth.

Am I saying that every local gathering should have all five expressions function all of the time? While I see multiplicity of leadership in scripture, I do not see the presence of all five of these graces as a requirement. However, if it is possible to have the impartation and release of all five graces all of the time, why not?! If all five are resident, it will not be necessary to shop around for impartation. We will not have to wait for a visiting ministry to bring a "little dab'll do ya" impartation to just get us by. Neither will it be necessary to chase around to conferences, hoping to leave equipped to function as we should. Having all five expressions of Christ present and released in a local gathering would provide a fast track where believers can be catapulted into being taught, trained, and activated to quickly begin administering the Kingdom, doing the greater works, and being a full expression of Christ in the earth!

Therefore, the second reason this content is worth our time is because . . .

WE WANT ALL BELIEVERS TO BECOME A COMPLETE EXPRESSION OF CHRIST IN THE EARTH.

Lastly, what does it mean when we call ourselves apostolic? Does it mean we are all apostles? Does it mean we should all aspire to grow up one day and be apostles because they are the greatest? Does it mean that an apostle should be the boss of us? No, to all of these.

Being an apostolic assembly means we are a place of sending. It is a place where believers are taught, trained, activated, and sent out. It means our focus is on the fulfillment of individual assignments given by Yahweh for the purpose of reclaiming territory for His Kingdom. It is a place of sending out locally, nationally, and internationally into whatever assignment one is given.

In conclusion, we see the emerging ecclesia of Yahweh to be a place where, with the operation of the five graces Christ gave, believers are taught, trained, activated, and sent out to fulfill the assignment they have been given in the earth.

CHAPTER ONE
EMBRACING THE FULL EXPRESSION OF CHRIST

Since the latter part of the last century, the church has been hearing undercurrents of conversation concerning the fivefold graces spoken of in Ephesians 4. We have even had occasional encounters with those promoting the operation of the fivefold graces in the church. There have also been occasions wherein those who might have been somewhat overzealous to have the five graces resident in their local fellowships have placed people in those positions in order to have them filled. This was done perhaps in the sincere attempt to simply establish what the fellowship believed to be right. The problem with this is that too often people who were not chosen by Yahweh for these assignments were placed in positions they were never meant to fill.

As with any restored revelation brought to the church by Yahweh, the pendulum often swings as far in one direction as it has been in the other before it finds itself settled in its true center, and so it is concerning the five graces Christ gave the church. We have been so eager to institute the restoration of order in the church that we have seen an apostle and a prophet around every corner and in our eagerness to be involved in the frontier of church restoration we have placed unjust expectations on men Yahweh never called to serve as such. This has created confusion and has brought a reproach on the true restoration of these gifts of Christ.

In recent years there has been somewhat of a settling of the confusion. It is as though men and women of reasonable minds have had encounters with Yahweh and have been jolted into the seriousness of the time we are in and the importance of the restoration of the order of Yahweh in the Ecclesia. Denominational boundaries are being crossed as even those in established religious order are beginning to inquire as to the function of the five graces in the church.

Many of the people of God are moving away from a position-related understanding of what we have known as church order and are embracing an orientation toward unique function. There exists sincere desire in the hearts of God's people to see the church become the world-changing entity it was designed to be. No longer are men satisfied to believe that the "greater things than these" works are meant for some other time, for some other people. Nor do they believe that those words were simply an overzealous expression by One, the Christ, who did not comprehend what the world would become.

People are asking, "Why not now?! Why not me?!" Yahweh is answering. He is restoring the five graces to their proper function:

> And He Himself gave some to be apostles, some prophets, some evangelists, and some pastors and teachers for the equipping of the saints for the work of ministry, for the edifying of the body of Christ, till we all come to the unity of the faith and the knowledge of the Son of God, to a perfect man to the measure of the stature of the fullness of Christ. (Ephesians 4: 11–13 NKJ)

That the saints might be equipped! The saints have been ill-equipped due to the lack of the five graces functioning properly in the church. That is simply the way things have been.

Things are changing. The five ministry graces are being restored. We need to understand what this means. We need to understand how this change impacts the body of Christ and each of us individually. It is in an effort to bring clarity and insight to these thoughts that I am writing. This is not an all-inclusive final word on the subject. It is simply a turning of new ground in preparation for planting of a tremendous harvest in our lives and in the lives of those around us.

Why the Fivefold?

The first question that must be answered is that of why we need the fivefold graces in the church. We have all likely heard or even said things such as: "Have we not done without them for years? Were not the twelve Apostles the only ones? After they died there were no more, right? Prophets are not for today! We have had priests and pastors for hundreds of years! What has been wrong with doing it the way we have done it for hundreds of years? The church has been doing fine just like it is! Leave it alone!" This is only a small sample of the statements we hear in opposition to the restoration of the five gifts of Christ in Ephesians 4.

The question of the existence of apostles and prophets in the earth today being one which has been more than adequately addressed, it will not be further explored here. Suffice it to say that this writing embraces the premise that indeed apostles and prophets do function in the earth today along with evangelists, pastors, and teachers.

The question then is whether or not the church, as we know it, is doing just fine and should be left alone to continue as it is. I am not addressing any particular denomination or set of denominational doctrine. I am asking whether or not that which Christ died and rose again to establish is functioning in the earth. Are the "greater works than these" that He said believers would do the norm or the exception?

The answer is glaring! While there are pockets in the earth and occasional outpourings where miracles, signs, and wonders take place, it is certainly not the norm. The church does not operate as though it truly believes that it has the authority to do the things Jesus did, such as heal the sick (Matthew 9:20–22), raise the dead (Mark 5:35–42), change the form of matter (John 2:5–9), or see miraculous provision (Matthew 17:27). These works are not commonplace, much less are the greater works Jesus spoke of in John 14:12 (NKJ):

> Truly, truly I say to you, he who believes in Me, the works that I do he will do also and greater works than these he will do because I go to My Father.

Demonstrations of service and self-sacrifice for our fellow man are seen in times of great disaster but are accompanied by vans and food trucks with church identifications prominently displayed in order to ensure that proper credit is received. We love those who agree with us and shun those who do not. We expect people to look right, sound right, and act right. We have become a religious bunch for sure, but are we the church Christ died for? Certainly not! We will not be as long as we fail to embrace the full expression of Christ in the earth.

CHAPTER TWO
AS ONE

Jesus said, "If you have known Me, you have known My Father" (John 14:7 NKJ). He is the complete expression of Yahweh. Yes, "God is Love," but He is so much more than what we understand love to be. I do not mean to be sacrilegious when I say that we have focused too much on love while ignoring the fullness of who Yahweh is as Love. Truly, we fall short in the area of love, but I believe two things to be true. First, we have had a wrong understanding of love. Second, the need for the church to complete its assignment in the earth has been crippled by its ongoing struggle to get this one thing right.

Struggling, striving to get any one thing right comes out of a works-based mentality. Whether it is waiting to serve God until you get your life sorted out, waiting to share the word of the Lord until your children stop misbehaving, or waiting until you have perfected love before you say yes to what Yahweh is asking you to do, you will live a life of waiting because there will always be a reason to keep waiting.

We can never work to be good enough. There is nothing we can do to arrive at being ready to do what He calls us to do. Wherever we are, in whatever condition, if God gives us instructions, we are only asked to obey. We are not asked to get right then obey. We forget that He knows everything, including our personal condition, reasons, and stories when He asks something of us. We must stop making things all about us!

Suffice it to say that our understanding of love as an emotion is very limited—not that emotion is not part of Yahweh. We see in Jesus anger and compassion, both of which are emotions. There is a time to weep and a time to laugh (Ecclesiastes 3:4). Emotion is part of us as it is part of Him. However, emotion is not to determine our obedience to purpose.

If not emotion, what is this love we are to manifest? For the purpose of this writing, I will define love as the willingness to be spent on behalf of someone else. It is the willingness to be used up, to expend oneself in whatever way God asks, for whatever purpose He asks, and for whomever He asks. This requires no emotion. It requires no "feeling" ready or able. It only requires obedience. This is the love that God is. Are we not fortunate that He does not have to be emotionally pleased with us in order to do what He has said He will do? Therefore, let us move from trying to get love right to being obedient as an expression of His love and of our love for Him.

If it is not just God's love that we learn from knowing Christ, what else can we know? In what other ways is Christ an expression of the Father? And, in what ways are we to be expressions of Him? This is where the five graces in Ephesians 4 enter the picture. Christ said He gave these for the equipping of the saints. Therefore, these will be referred to as the gifts of Christ. Christ gave apostles, prophets, evangelists, pastors, and teachers. All are recognized and valued as essential entities for the success of the establishment of the Kingdom of Yahweh on the Earth.

What is Ephesians 4:11–13 saying to us?

"And He Himself gave . . ."

There is no question concerning who the Giver is in the transaction. Christ, Himself, the One who first descended then ascended and is seated at the right of Father, gave these five expressions of Himself to the receiver, the church. Being the greatest expression of the apostle, prophet, evangelist, pastor and teacher, He left these expressions of Himself to the church in order that the church might be a continued expression of Him in the earth.

" . . . for the equipping of the saints . . ."

What does it mean that the saints, the set-apart ones, the believers, are to be equipped? The word translated as "equipping" is *katartismo* (Gk) and would be better translated as "perfecting." Its meaning is: "to bring into full maturity" or "to make fully fit" (Vines, 847).

How is one brought to full maturity or made fully fit for an assignment? Is it by textbook instruction alone? Would we want our surgeons to operate on us after only classroom instruction? Most certainly not! Being brought to full maturity requires being taught, trained, and activated. When one is taught, he is instructed in truth. Training involves demonstration of truth and activation refers to the release of the student to operate in that which he has been taught and trained. The responsibility for doing this was placed squarely on the shoulders of the apostle, prophet, evangelist, pastor, and teacher.

" . . . FOR THE WORK OF THE MINISTRY . . ."

What is the work of the ministry? We can establish that this does not refer to works or obligatory duties. Work refers to any task undertaken. *Diakonia* (Vines, 746) which is translated "ministry" could also have been translated "administration," hence, "for the work of the administration." Immediately, our minds open to new understanding.

In ancient times, the *diakonia* was actually a storehouse supervised by the government in which provisions for the needy were held and from which they were distributed. Those who were assigned to this task were called *diakonos,* or ministers. Their goal was to offer provisions in order to assist those less fortunate in becoming contributing citizens.

To this point, then, we could say that Christ gave expressions of Himself that they might teach, train, and activate all believers in their assigned tasks in order that all believers might become contributing citizens in the Kingdom. In other words, apostles, prophets, evangelists, pastors, and teachers have been given the assignment to teach, train, and activate all believers to be administrators of the Kingdom of God on earth. By doing so, all believers, including apostles, prophets, evangelists, pastors, and teachers, are thereby given the tools necessary to fulfill their assignment. All believers are to be *diakonos,* that is, ministers or administrators of their assignment.

" . . . FOR THE EDIFYING OF THE BODY OF CHRIST . . ."

Oikodome (Vines, 347–348), translated "edifying" or "building," is used in reference to increasing in spiritual maturity. It calls to mind the image of a systematic, gradual construction of a sound structure. First, the good foundation, then the frame, followed by the roof and so forth, with each component being carefully added at the appropriate time, in the appropriate manner. The structure being built is the body of Christ, the Ecclesia of Yahweh, not to be confused with any denomination or man-designed institution.

" . . . UNTIL . . ."

"Until?" Have we arrived at the "until"? Have we arrived at the time in which the saints have been equipped to do what they are assigned to do? We have not reached that point. Therefore, all that is included in Ephesians 4 remains relevant.

" . . . WE ALL COME TO THE UNITY OF THE FAITH AND THE KNOWLEDGE OF THE SON OF GOD . . ."

This does not say, "until we all come to agree on the doctrines of a denomination." What is this faith that is universal? What is this faith in which we may all be one? Is it acknowledgement of Jesus as Messiah? This cannot be the answer, for many who acknowledge this intellectually are not part of the one body of Christ. Neither is it holding His promises or His word as an anchor for life, for many who do so remain unable to walk together as the one body of Christ. What is the one common thread that has the ability to make one of many people? This common thread is simply trusting Yeshua the Messiah, the Son of God. This is the point of agreement we should operate from.

" . . . TO A PERFECT MAN, TO THE MEASURE OF THE STATURE OF THE FULLNESS OF CHRIST . . ."

All of this is done in order that the church, the Ecclesia of Yahweh, might be a mature expression of Christ. In other words, Christ gave some to be apostles, prophets, evangelists, pastors, and teachers. When He gave them, He assigned them the task to teach, train, and activate all believers to be administrators of the Kingdom of God on earth. This training was to impart to them everything necessary to complete their assignments on earth. In this way, all believers are to become contributing, mature citizens who can walk **_AS ONE_** sound structure and full expression of Christ in the earth.

CONCLUSION

Until we come to a common understanding of our faith, we as believers are to be taught, trained and activated in all things necessary for the administration of His Kingdom. This preparation is the responsibility of apostles, prophets, evangelists, pastors, and teachers to whom Jesus gave the assignment. These are not positions or titles that can be claimed or appointed by man. They are assignments that should be approached with awe and fear of the One who issues the command.

In order to be fully equipped to be a complete expression of Christ, we must receive impartation from all five gifts that Christ gave. To only receive from one, two, or even three of them leaves us lacking in the expression of the others. This means we would be only a partial expression of Christ Himself. Is that what we want? Is this what we are meant to be? I believe that a large part of the reason the church has not been accomplishing her assignment in the earth is because she has been denied access to becoming the full expression of Christ.

CHAPTER THREE
ON COMMON GROUND

Just as having a common understanding of Ephesians 4:11–13 is necessary for correct communication, other terms and concepts also need to be made clear. Miscommunication is the enemy's playground; therefore, we desire to make our communication clear.

OUR ASSIGNMENT

> Then God blessed them and God said to them, "Be fruitful and multiply; fill the earth and subdue it; have dominion over the fish of the sea, over the birds of the air, and over every living thing that moves on the earth." (Genesis 1:28 NKJ)

This is the assignment God gave man. It has not changed. Man's right to operate in the authority he was given was lost when Adam and Eve disobeyed the instruction God gave them in the

Garden. Jesus came and restored that authority to us. Our assignment remains the same.

The assignment has three parts:

1. Be fruitful and multiply
2. Fill the earth and subdue it
3. Have dominion over the fish of the sea, over the birds of the air, and over every living thing that moves on the earth

"BE FRUITFUL AND MULTIPLY, FILL THE EARTH AND SUBDUE IT . . ."

The being fruitful and multiplying has not been a problem in the physical realm. The first man, Adam, however, failed in his assignment to multiply himself as a likeness of God in the earth, created in His own image.

The idea of subduing has grown to conjure such a negative image in our minds. Subdue does not mean to whip into shape, to force into submission, or to rule with an iron fist. To subdue actually comes from an old agricultural term meaning to "bring into maximum productivity or fruitfulness." What a shift that understanding brings in our thinking! That is our responsibility over the earth. We are to bring it into its maximum productivity or fruitfulness.

" . . . HAVE DOMINION . . ."

Very simply, to have dominion means to rule over something.

As a royal priesthood (1 Peter 2:9 NKJ), we have been made "kings" and priests" (Revelations 1:6 NKJ) and as such have not only the right but the responsibility to rule over the earth. When Adam disobeyed, all of mankind lost his right and authority to rule. He lost access to the One who had given the assignment, but the assignment never has changed. The entire written word is simply the story of Yahweh's desire to restore the original order He established for His Kingdom. May His Kingdom come, His will be done, on earth as it is already being done in Heaven!

THE MESSAGE

What is our message to be? Our message should be the same one Jesus carried:

> From that time Jesus began to preach and to say, "Repent, for the kingdom of heaven is at hand." (Matthew 4:17 NKJ)

His message was of the Kingdom. So should our message be. It was for this purpose He was sent:

> But He said to them, "I must preach the kingdom of God to the other cities also, because for this purpose I have been sent." (Luke 4:43 NKJ)

Grace and Function

In reference to the apostle, prophet, evangelist, pastor, and teacher listed in Ephesians 4:11, we have often heard them referred to as offices. The term "office" brings to mind the idea of rank and position. Rank is a recognition awarded for performance. Surely we do not serve a God who issues assignments as time goes by based on performance of individuals deemed deserving. Who among us would ever be deserving? I do not embrace the concept of rank in the church. However, I do embrace that there is an important and necessary order of assembly that is required for successful function. I believe that this lack of accurate assembly has had a crippling affect on the church fulfilling her Genesis 1 assignment.

Rank automatically makes me think of one thing being more important than another or of one thing dominating another. This seems to be a positional perspective. We are not concerned with the position of the apostle, prophet, evangelist, pastor, or teacher, but rather their function. Function refers to one's operation in the assignment he has been given. For this reason, I will not use the traditional terminology of "office" but will instead use the terms "grace" and "function" when referencing the apostle, prophet, teacher, evangelist, and pastor.

Grace, or *charis* (Vines, 500), means power and equipping for ministry. Paul understood that he had received power and equipping to be an apostle:

> Paul, a servant of Jesus Christ, called to be an apostle . . . (Romans 1:1)

> Nevertheless, brethren, I have written more boldly to you on some points, as reminding you, because of the grace given to me by God. (Romans 15:15 NKJ)

> If indeed you have heard of the dispensation of the grace of God which was given to me for you . . . (Ephesians 3:2 NKJ)

> Of which I became a minister according to the gift of the grace of God given to me by the effective working of His power. (Ephesians 3:7 NKJ)

This power and equipping he had received was recognized by others:

> And when James, Cephas, and John, who seemed to be pillars perceived the grace that had been given to me . . . (Galatians 2:9 NKJ)

Paul and others understood that he was given power and equipping for a specific assignment:

> That we should go to the Gentiles . . . (Galatians 2:9 NKJ)

Therefore, when I say evangelistic grace, for example, I am saying that someone has been given the power and equipping necessary to function as an evangelist. They have been supernaturally enabled to exemplify that particular expression of Christ in the earth. In other words, that person has been divinely given grace for his function.

WILLY-NILLY?!

If we do not want to think in terms of rank or position, does this mean we are all willy-nilly, having no order or chain of command? Are we an army in disarray? This cannot be correct! We might ask who is in charge or who is the most important? The answers are simple: Yahweh is in charge. He is the most important. If we keep Him and His plan at the forefront, we will begin to see ourselves as servants of our King instead of servants of a doctrine, denomination, man, or of ourselves.

If we attempt to assign greater importance to one of the five graces over the others, it is as if we are saying one expression of Christ is more important than the others. We know this is not true. This, again, is why it is so important that the body receive impartation from all five of the graces. In this way, every believer is equipped to be whatever expression of Christ is needed at a particular time.

This does not mean there is no order of authority. Authority comes with assignment. Assignment defines one's sphere of responsibility. With that sphere of responsibility comes the authority to complete the assignment. The President of the United States has a vast, far-reaching assignment with great responsibility and authority. But, that authority and responsibility does not reach into my home. My home is outside of his sphere of responsibility.

He has no authority in my home.

While we embrace the priesthood of all believers and see all believers as being of equal importance, we do also embrace the principle of *primo inter pares* or "first among equals." We believe in equality as sons of God, agreeing that no one is better, more important, or more valuable than any other. However, we do acknowledge that there is not equality of function. There are various degrees of ability, various degrees of responsibility, and various degrees of grace (power and equipping for ministry), depending on the requirements of the assignment given.

In a group, large or small, there will be one who rises as first among equals by God's design. This does not exalt him above others but places him in a position of greater responsibility. This person might be described as "chief" or "eminent" as we see eminent apostles spoken of in 2 Corinthians 12:11, or chief priests spoken of in Luke 9:22. This simply means that this person is the one who will be held accountable to God for the assignment.

Conclusion

- The term function will be used to refer to a person's operation in the assignment he has been given.
- The term grace will be used to refer to the power and equipping for ministry a person receives in conjunction with his assignment.
- All five graces—apostle, prophet, evangelist, pastor, and teacher—are equally important as expressions of Christ given to equip believers to be administrators of

the Kingdom of God on earth.
- With an assignment comes authority and responsibility for that assignment.
- Among the many who are equal, there will be a first or chief among, not above, those equals who is chosen by Yahweh to be held to account.

CHAPTER FOUR
THE APOSTOLIC GRACE

What does it mean when we say that someone has the grace of an apostle? What does it mean when we say that someone has the power and equipping to be administrators of the Kingdom of God on earth as an apostle? What does it mean to say that someone operates in the function of an apostle? What does it mean that this person operates as an expression of Christ? What does an apostle carry which he is to impart to believers? First we must consider the meaning of the word "apostle," then we will consider the One who demonstrated the meaning.

The word apostle is derived from the Greek term *apostolos*, which has come to mean, "one sent forth." This word, *apostolos*, was originally a nautical term which referred to either a fleet of ships which was sent on an assignment, the commander of the fleet that was sent, or even the assignment itself after completion. In other words, it could be said that an *apostolos* was commissioned to lead an *apostolos* to complete an *apostolos*. This meaning has been reduced to mean, "one sent forth."

In the Aramaic English New Testament, Ephesians 4:11 does not use the word apostle but rather "schlichim." This word would be better translated in English to "emissary," which is the word also used in the Complete Jewish Bible. Therefore, what does it mean to be an emissary?

An emissary is a person who is sent on a mission to represent another person or organization. It is one who is the designated agent or representative of another. As such, he goes under the authority of the sender, carries the message of the sender, and is accountable to the sender. All things relate back to the sender. We conclude then that the one referred to as an apostle in Ephesians 4:11 is one who goes out under the authority of the Sender, who carries the message of the Sender, and who is accountable to the Sender. He is more than just a messenger. He is the likeness and image of the Sender, is expected to act as such and to be received as such.

Christ our Example

Christ, as the only infallible Apostle, is our example:

> Therefore, holy brethren, partakers of the heavenly calling, consider the Apostle and High Priest of our confession, Christ Jesus. (Hebrews 3:1 NKJ)

Jesus was sent by God and spoke God's words:

> For God did not send His Son into the world to

condemn the world but that the world through Him might be saved. (John 3:17 NKJ)

For He whom God has sent speaks the words of God . . .(John 3:34 NKJ)

And the Father Himself, who sent Me . . . (John 5:37 NKJ)

Jesus answered and said to them, "This is the work of God, that you believe in Him whom He sent." (John 6:29 NKJ)

But I know Him, for I am from Him, and He sent Me. (John 7:29 NKJ)

Jesus was given an assignment:

But I have a greater witness than John's for the works which the Father has given Me to finish—the very works that I do—bear witness of Me, that the Father has sent Me (John 5:36 NKJ)

Jesus operated under the authority of the One who sent Him:

I can of Myself do nothing. As I hear, I judge; and My judgment is righteous, because I do not seek

My own will but the will of the Father who sent Me (John 5:30 NKJ)

Jesus fully demonstrated what it is to be an apostle or emissary. He went out under the authority of the Sender. He carried the word and did the works of the Sender. He behaved like the Sender and did what the Sender would do. He spoke and acted like the Sender. An emissary speaks and acts in such a way that, upon his departure, those left behind have the impression that they have been in the presence of the Sender.

> Jesus said, "For I have not spoken on My own authority; but the Father who sent Me gave Me a command, what I should say and what I should speak." (John 12:49 NKJ)

We can justify concluding that everything Jesus did, He did as an Apostle or Emissary. He taught, He healed, He met needs—all as an Apostle on assignment and under the authority of His Father. Also, He was aware that He would return to His Father to account for the assignment.

This leads us to the questions of what His assignment was. Was His assignment to seek and save that which was lost? Was His assignment to heal the sick and to set the captives free? Was His assignment to make a way for us to have life and that more abundantly? Was His assignment to make it possible to do greater works than those which He did? He did all of these, but were these things His assignment? No. These were manifestations or demonstrations of His assignment. His assignment can be found in Luke 4:43 (NKJ):

> But He said to them, "I must preach the kingdom of God to the other cities also, because for this purpose I have been sent."

> But He said to them, "I must announce the Good News of the Kingdom of God to the other towns too—this is why I was sent." (Complete Jewish Bible)

Through the years, I have heard many people express the desire to just find a good church where they preach Jesus Christ and Him crucified. When I hear this it is as though I hear Jesus scream, "NOOOOOOOOOO!" Do not misunderstand. I am not making light of that message, for indeed, there is no other Name by which men might be saved. Without this message we would not be having this conversation. However, Jesus did not suffer, die, and rise again just so men could be saved from Hell and go to a place called Heaven! All that Jesus did was done in order that those who would believe in Him might become citizen warriors of the Kingdom and pick up the assignment to restore Kingdom order to the earth where He left off.

So then, should our message be to tell people about Jesus, lead them through the Door of salvation then immediately introduce Him as King? In other words, do we share the gospel of salvation then share the gospel of the Kingdom? Certainly not! There are not two gospels! While the idea of doing this might seem to be progressive thought, it continues to embrace a division of the truth. There is only one gospel and that is the gospel of the Kingdom of which the message of salvation is a necessary part.

Why not present the truth from the beginning as in Genesis 1? God created all things. On the sixth day He created man. When He placed them on earth, He gave them an assignment along with everything they would need for the assignment. Man had open communication with God. All was well. In time, man lost his right of dominion on the earth by committing treason. Open communication with God was broken. All of the written word is the story of God's plan to restore this original order in the earth. At the appointed time, Jesus entered the physical world. His assignment was to announce the Good News of the Kingdom and make a way for man's right of dominion to be restored. This He did by teaching and demonstrating the way the Kingdom is intended to operate and by becoming the Door through which man might leave captivity in the kingdom of darkness and enter the Kingdom of God. Upon entering the Kingdom, one becomes not just a subject to be cared for by the King but a warrior in the army of the Lord with the responsibility to see His Kingdom come, His will be done on earth as it is in heaven! This is the awesome truth!

Everything Jesus did and said is connected with restoration of the Kingdom. He turned the tables over in the temple, declaring that His Father's house was not to be a "house of merchandise!" (John 2:14–16 NKJ) but rather a "house of prayer" (Matthew 21:12–13 NKJ). He brought Kingdom order. It was not always pretty. He fed the 5000, demonstrating that, in the Kingdom, the

King provides. He appeared out of nowhere. He defied the laws of nature by walking on water and controlling weather. He commanded matter to change form, turning water into wine. All of these were demonstrations of the way the Kingdom is supposed to operate. These are demonstrations. The assignment was restoration of the Kingdom. We have too long reveled in the demonstrations without embracing the assignment.

This leaves us still asking, "What is the function of the apostle? What is the apostle's assignment?" To answer this question, we must consider the commission given to the eleven disciples by the Apostle Christ:

> Then Jesus came and spoke to them saying, "All authority has been given to Me in heaven and on earth. Go therefore and make disciples of all the nations, baptizing them in the name of the Father and of the Son and of the Holy Spirit, teaching them to observe all things that I have commanded you; and lo, I am with you always, even to the end of the age." (Matthew 28:18–20 NKJ)

What does it mean, "to make disciples"? In the original language of Jesus, Aramaic, the word translated here as disciples is *talmidim*. This word refers to much more than just followers or ones who are disciplined. In the Jewish educational system of that time, boys and girls ages four to twelve attended Bet Sefer in a synagogue. Their education consisted of learning to read and write using one textbook, the Torah, which they were charged to memorize.

From ages thirteen to fifteen, the very best of the male students were selected to continue their education. Their education consisted of memorizing the Tanach while learning the trade of their family. This level of education is Bet Midrash.

The final level of education, Bet Talmud, was reserved for only the best of the best students. Entrance to the Bet Talmud was by invitation of the rabbi only. This education took place from ages fifteen to thirty and led to the possibility of becoming a rabbi. This level of education required much more than a casual following around or learning teachings. The goal was to become so close a reflection of the rabbi that when the *talmidim*, as the student was called, was seen, all would know who his rabbi was because he looked, spoke, and acted just like his rabbi. In training, the students would eat what the rabbi ate, sleep when the rabbi slept, dress as the rabbi dressed, move the way the rabbi moved, and learn to think and understand Torah the way the rabbi did. It was said that they were to "walk in the dust of their rabbi." This gave reference to the fact that they walked so closely behind their rabbi that the dust thrown up by the rabbi's steps would cover them. This walking referred to their entire existence. Ones who achieved this level of education were called *talmidim*. The eleven disciples, who were themselves *talmidim*, were commissioned by Jesus to make *talmidim* in all nations.

These *talmidim* were charged to make *talmidim* of all nations, teaching them to observe all things they had been taught. Observe, or keep, is translated from the word *tereo*, which means to watch over, preserve, or watch. They were commanded to do so. Commanded is translated from the *entello,* which means to enjoin upon or charge with. They were to teach others to preserve all of what they had been charged with. This was a command with no end and is therefore as applicable today as it was the day Jesus spoke it.

In Mark 16: 15 we see this command:

> And He said to them, "Go into all the world and preach the <u>gospel</u> to every creature."

They were commanded to preach, or *evangelion,* the gospel, or good news. We see this same word used in Acts 20:24 (NKJ):

> But none of these things move me; nor do I count my life dear to myself, so that I may finish my race with joy, and the ministry which I received from the Lord Jesus, to testify to the <u>gospel</u> of the grace of God.

And I Peter 4:17 (NKJ):

> For the time has come for judgment to begin at the house of God; and if it begins with us first, what will be the end of those who do not obey the <u>gospel</u> of God?

> But He said to them, 'I must preach the kingdom of God to the other cities also, because for this

purpose I have been sent. (Luke 4:43 CJB)

What did Jesus teach that they were to preserve? He taught, in word and deed, the restoration of the Kingdom. They were to do the same. The assignment they were left with was to teach, train, and activate believers in the operation and order of Kingdom life. The apostle has been given the particular grace (power and equipping) necessary to accomplish this assignment. He has been given the authority to do it. He has been given the responsibility to do it.

The obvious question is whether we are all not responsible for seeing the Kingdom established. We most certainly are. If you want to be the most effective you can be, however, it is necessary that you connect whatever your assignment is with the apostolic grace. The apostolic grace carries the responsibility for imparting the order and authority of the Kingdom message. This in no way elevates the apostle above the other graces or any individual believer. It is simply to acknowledge and allow the operation of the assigned function of the apostle in order to accomplish the assignment Christ released on the earth.

CHOOSING THE TWELVE

How do we see this demonstrated in the New Testament apostles?

> Now it came to pass in those days that He went out to the mountain to pray, and continued all night in prayer to God. And when it was day, He called His disciples to Him; and from them He chose twelve

whom He also named apostles. Simon, whom He also named Peter, and Andrew his brother; James and John; Philip and Bartholomew; Matthew and Thomas; James the son of Alpaeus, and Simon called the Zealot; Judas the son of James, and Judas Iscariot who also became a traitor. (Luke 6:12–16 NKJ)

He spent the night in prayer receiving instructions from His Father. He only did what His Father told him to do. In other words, who actually chose the twelve? Father chose the twelve. Consider the following translation from the Complete Jewish Bible:

It was around that time that Yeshua went out to the hill country to pray, and all night he continued in prayer to God. When day came he called his *talmidim* and chose from among them twelve to be known as emissaries. (Luke 6:12–13)

Talmidim . . . emissaries . . . Recall that an emissary is a person who is sent on a mission to represent another person or organization. Also, recall that a *talmidim* is supposed to represent his rabbi to such a great extent that for all who see him, it will be as if they have actually seen the rabbi. Each of the twelve apostles was first a *talmidim*. It was from among *talmidim* that emissaries, or apostles, were chosen.

What were the twelve apostles assigned to do? They were to

continue His assignment, i.e., restore the Kingdom. They were to do what He did and even more (John 14:12). As *talmidim*, they were to speak as He would speak. As emissaries, or apostles, they were to carry His authority. In essence, they were to "be" Him. They were to look and sound like Him. They were indeed *talmidim* who were given the specific assignment to be emissaries or apostles.

We see examples of how the New Testament apostles successfully mirrored Christ. Peter demonstrated the Kingdom:

> Acts 5: passed judgment
> Acts 3: healed the lame man
> Acts 9: raised Dorcas from the dead

Apostles brought Kingdom order and commissioned men for service in their Kingdom assignments:

> Then the twelve summoned the multitude of the disciples and said, 'It is not desirable that we should leave the word of God and serve tables. Therefore, brethren, seek out from among you seven men of good reputation, full of the Holy Spirit and wisdom, whom we may appoint over this business; but we will give ourselves continually to prayer and to the ministry of the word. And the saying pleased the whole multitude. And they chose Stephen, a man full of faith and the Holy Spirit and Philip, Prochorus, Nicanor, Timon, Parmenas, and Nicolas, a proselyte

THE APOSTOLIC GRACE

from Antioch . . . (Acts 6:2–5 NKJ)

Those who were commissioned then went out and performed signs, wonders, and mighty deeds as they shared the Kingdom message.

CONSIDER

Jesus was sent by the Father. He was an emissary of the Father. He was to represent the Father, say what the Father said, and do what the Father did. Also: "He who has seen Me has seen the Father" (John 14:9 NKJ).

It was as if Jesus was saying that He was an exact representation of His Father.

Jesus had *talmidim*, disciples, who were to be like Him and represent Him in all ways. They were to do what He did and even more, and say what He said. They were to be exact representations of Him.

From these *talmidim*, He chose the twelve Father said to choose and commissioned them as emissaries, apostles, with the charge to continue His assignment (Luke 4:43) the way He would do it. What was this assignment?

> But He said to them, "I must preach the kingdom of God to the other cities also, because for this purpose I have been sent." (Luke 4:43 NKJ)

As extensions of Christ, they were to assume the responsibility for continuing His assignment. The assignment of the apostle has not changed. He is to preach the gospel of the Kingdom and demonstrate the way the Kingdom is supposed to operate on earth. He is to impart this understanding and authority for establishing order to all believers in order that all believers might then establish that order and exercise that authority in the sphere of influence that is their assignment.

THE NECESSITY

Restoration of the apostolic grace to its proper function among believers is necessary for the restoration of the Kingdom of God on Earth. Why? It is necessary because restoration of Kingdom order and authority is the grace the apostles carry. This is the power and equipping for ministry that they carry and which they are to impart to believers. It is their assignment. It is their responsibility. They have the authority to accomplish the assignment. It is necessary that the apostolic grace be locked into its proper function in order for the Kingdom of God to be restored on the earth.

EVIDENCE

What then is the evidence that someone carries the apostolic grace? Is it that they perform miracles, signs, and wonders? Although these are evidences which accompany an apostle, they should also follow all who are believers. Is it that they should be knowledgeable in God's word, wise concerning His ways, and a true reflection of Him? Yes, they should, but so should all *talmidim* be. Is it that they found local churches? Should we be able to point to different locations around the world and credit a certain person with establishing those works? Is one who establishes more "works" around the world a more powerful apostle? In fact, we do not see evidence that this is a required proof that one is an apostle.

What we do see is that a true apostle has taken up the assignment given to him to share the message of the Kingdom in word and in deed and see the Kingdom come on earth as it is in heaven. Apostles will not be focused on the growth of a local church organization. He will not be focused on promoting a denominational doctrine. Their focus will be to see the Kingdom of God restored in order and authority. That is the grace, the power and equipping, they carry to impart to all believers. As an apostle takes his place and begins functioning in his assignment, the understanding of Kingdom order and authority will be imparted to all believers. All believers then, having been taught, trained, and activated in Kingdom order, will be able to exercise their Kingdom authority to establish this order in the assignment they have been given.

For example, a father who understands kingdom order will be equipped to establish this order as he operates in apostolic authority in guiding his family. A mother who understands Kingdom order will be equipped to establish this order as she operated in apostolic authority in her assigned sphere of responsibility. Even the children who understand Kingdom order will be able to establish that order in their sphere of influence, even if that sphere only involves their homework, chores, or pets. In like manner, a teacher will be able to establish Kingdom order in her classroom through the exercise of apostolic authority. An employer or employee will be able to exercise Kingdom authority to establish

Kingdom order in their sphere of responsibility or influence. The list goes on.

Every believer, regardless of age, location, or station in life, has a sphere of influence and responsibility or assignment. Therefore, every believer, having received an impartation of the apostolic grace, has a responsibility to exercise that grace for the purpose of seeing His Kingdom come in order and authority on earth as it is in Heaven. It is the assignment or responsibility of the apostle to impart to all believers the grace he has been given in order to see this happen.

CHAPTER FIVE
THE PROPHETIC GRACE

According to the word, all may prophesy:

> But this is what was spoken by the prophet Joel: "And it shall come to pass in the last days, says God, That I will pour out of My Spirit on all flesh; Your sons and your daughters shall prophesy." (Acts 2:16–17 NKJ)

All should desire to prophesy:

> Pursue love, and desire spiritual gifts, but especially that you may prophesy. (I Cor 14:1 NKJ)

However, all are not prophets. Neither should all desire to be prophets. It is not ours to assume an assignment, sphere of influence, or responsibility, but rather to receive the assignment chosen for us by Yahweh. However, as we saw with the apostle, as one of the five expressions of Himself that Christ gave the church for its equipping, all believers may receive an impartation and activation of the prophetic grace from those who carry it. In the same manner in which a prophet is empowered and equipped to be an administrator of the Kingdom of God on the earth, he may impart this expression or grace to all believers that they might exercise this expression of Christ as needed.

Prophecy is one of the nine gifts given to believers by Holy Spirit:

> Now there are diversities of gifts, but the same Spirit. There are differences of ministries, but the same Lord. And there are diversities of activities, but it is the same God who works all in all. But the manifestation of the Spirit is given to each one for the profit of all: for to one is given the word of wisdom through the Spirit , to another the word of knowledge through the same Spirit, to another faith by the same Spirit, to another gifts of healing by the same Spirit, to another the working of miracles, to another prophecy, to another discerning of spirits, to another different kinds of tongues, to another the interpretation of tongues. (1 Corinthians 12:4–10 NKJ)

This gift of prophecy is not to be confused with the prophetic grace given to some by Christ in Ephesians 4:11–13.

THE PROPHETIC GRACE

When I began to consider the prophet, and even when I asked others about the prophetic grace, thoughts generally were first expressed concerning what a prophet does. This most often leads into a discussion of the various manifestations that commonly accompany the prophetic grace. Then the question arose concerning whether or not these manifestations are evidence that one was a prophet. That cannot be true, because all of the manifestations of Holy Spirit are to be part of the life of every believer. I conclude then that our discussion should not be about what a prophet does but rather about who he is.

The assignment of a prophet is not to teach, train, and activate believers to do what he does but rather *to be* who he is as an expression of Christ. Our question then becomes, "Who is the prophet? What grace does he carry? What does he release into the atmosphere just by being present?" All he does will flow out of who he is.

I have a background in agriculture. I enjoy gardening and cooking. I also really enjoy baseball. My husband was a builder for years. Many of my references will relate to these areas because knowledge and understanding of these things is part of who I am. These are things I do that are part of me and affect my view of life and my communication. These things I do or have experience with, however, do not have as much effect on my response to life as does who I am, however. I am a teacher, an imparter of knowledge, a bringer of truth, an opener of the mind. If I am asked a question, I will seldom tell you the answer. I will first try to lead you to find the answer for yourself. Also, I feel compelled to share knowledge and information that I find interesting and valuable.

I love to learn and simply do not understand why everyone does not share my passion. This is the core of who I am. My views of life, my actions and reactions, can be traced back to this driving force in my life.

By the same token, who is a prophet? What is the basic motivation of a prophet? What drives him? What is at the core of who he is? In all of the variety of personalities and mannerisms, what is the common thread we can find running through the prophetic grace?

Old Testament Examples

The first mention we see of a prophet is of Abraham. God spoke of him:

> Now therefore, restore the man's wife; for he is a prophet. (Genesis 20:7 NKJ)

Moses was a great prophet. He knew God face to face. God gave him specific instructions concerning what he should say and do:

> But since then there has not arisen in Israel a prophet like Moses, whom the Lord knew face to face, in all the signs and wonders which the LORD sent him to do in the land of Egypt. (Deut. 34:10–11 NKJ)

Jeremiah was a prophet (Jeremiah 1:5–10). Ezekiel was a prophet (Ezekiel 2:1–5) And on it goes with other examples such as Hosea, Amos, Nahum, Elisha, and Elijah. We see that they were all raised up by God to hear what He was saying and speak on His behalf. They did not speak out of their own mind, emotion, and will, but rather according to what God said.

The Ultimate Example

Jesus is our ultimate example of the prophet as He only said what He heard His Father say. He was recognized as a prophet:

So the multitudes said, "This is Jesus, the prophet from Nazareth of Galilee."

> "But when they sought to lay hands on Him, they feared the multitudes, because they took Him for a prophet." (Matt 21:11, 46 NKJ)

> And He said to them, "What things?" And they said to Him, "The things concerning Jesus of Nazareth, who was a Prophet mighty in deed and word before God and all the people." (Luke 24:19 NKJ)

He received His words from His Father:

> I have many things to say and to judge concerning you, but He who sent Me is true; and I speak to the world those things which I heard from Him. (John 8:26 NKJ)

OTHER NEW TESTAMENT EXAMPLES

We see numerous examples of prophets in the New Testament. We see Silas and Judas:

> Now Judas and Silas, themselves being prophets also, exhorted the brethren with many words and strengthened them. (Acts 15:32 NKJ)

Certain prophets and teachers are mentioned:

> Now in the church that was at Antioch there were certain prophets and teachers: Barnabas, Simeon who was called Niger, Lucius of Cyrene, Manaen, who had been brought up with Herod the tetrarch, and Saul. (Acts 13:1 NKJ)

There were prophets who came from Jerusalem:

> And in these days prophets came from Jerusalem to Antioch. (Acts 11:27 NKJ)

Anna was a prophet:

> Now there was one, Anna, a prophetess . . , (Luke 2: 36 NKJ)

These are all examples of the prophet and his function or what he does. They speak and act in various ways. From what the prophet does, we see who he is.

What is the common thread that runs through all of these examples? This will tell us what drives them. This will identify their motivating force. The common thread is that they all saw and heard from God. They all spoke according to His direction. But, wait! Should not we all do that? Yes, we should and we can but those assigned to carry the grace of the prophet have been given this power and equipping for ministry as an expression of Christ to be imparted to believers. It is their responsibility to fulfill their assignment and impart this power and equipping for ministry to all believers. It is the responsibility of all believers to receive this impartation.

Prophets, like the apostles, have a focus on the Father. The apostle receives revelation of Kingdom structure and operation and is assigned to release that grace to all believers in order that they might do the same. Embracing this grace is part of what enables believers to be Kingdom citizens living in Kingdom structure and operation. The prophet receives revelation from Father concerning what Father is seeing and saying. He operates strongly in the revelation gifts of word of wisdom, word of knowledge, and discerning of spirits. He sees into spiritual dimensions. He decrees and declares destiny and potential over the earth. In short, he receives spiritual insight. This is the prophetic grace in operation. This is his function.

He does not carry this grace in order to be the big man in charge or the one who runs the show. He is but one expression of Christ, as are the others. To give him more value than others would be to devalue the others, and by doing so, devalue an expression of Christ Himself! May it never be so!

The prophet's assignment as an expression of Christ as one of the five graces in Ephesians 4 is to teach, train, and activate believers to hear and see into the Spirit realm. He is to impart the grace that comes from hearing and speaking His rhema word, to impart the faith to see and know the course of lives, nations, and events, and to impart the faith to decree and declare according to Father's directives. In other words, He is to equip believers to exercise their spiritual senses and to operate out of spiritual insight.

The purpose of this assignment is that the power and equipping for ministry that the prophet carries might be multiplied in the earth. As a result, instead of having a single spokesman for God scattered about here and there or over certain areas, there will be an army of Kingdom citizens who are spokesmen for Yahweh, hearing, seeing, decreeing, and declaring according to His will. All of this to the end of seeing His Kingdom come, His will be done, over the whole earth as it is in Heaven.

Apostles and prophets work well together. They both have their primary focus on the Father. It is not uncommon for apostles and prophets to be somewhat impatient with those unlike them. They can seem distant, callus, and arrogant. They consider that others should see things the way they do. This is not a bad thing. It is who they are. The frustration they experience with others will diminish as they begin to embrace their assignment to equip others in the prophetic grace rather than just expecting them to have understanding and operate in that grace. It is this failure to equip others, instead holding the grace as a personal possession that frustrates the apostle and prophet and the believers they are in contact with. When he begins to operate in his assignment to equip others, the prophet as well as the apostle will experience the joy of fulfilling his purpose. Believers, too, will find the joy of operating in proper order as Kingdom citizen warriors operating out of their spiritual senses.

Conclusion

The apostle imparts a passion for Kingdom order and authority. Under the impartation of the grace he carries, this passion will be stirred in believers to see His Kingdom come, His will be done, on earth as it is in Heaven. Believers will begin to have insight into a universal plan. Thoughts and actions will begin to reflect a new focus on seeing the establishment of His Kingdom order and authority.

The prophet imparts a passion to believers to have their eyes and ears opened to the spiritual realm. They begin to have great desire to hear and see into the spiritual realm and to actually participate in the administration of the Kingdom on earth out of this spiritual insight.

CHAPTER SIX
TAKE A BREATH

As I progress through this understanding, I find it necessary to regroup occasionally and remind myself of the first things, the place from which truth was given to man. In Genesis 1:28 we see that man was given an assignment:

> Then God blessed them, and God said to them, "Be fruitful and multiply; fill the earth and subdue it; have dominion over the fish of the sea, over the birds of the air, and over every living thing that moves on the earth." (Genesis 1:28 NKJ)

This assignment has three parts:

1. Be fruitful and multiply
2. Fill the earth and subdue it
3. Have dominion

At the time the assignment was given, man walked in constant, unhindered open communion with God as he fulfilled his assignment. The Kingdom was operating in perfect order.

Over time, an enemy arose. Man committed treason against the Kingdom, thereby abdicating his authority to fulfill his assignment. He lost constant, open communication with Yahweh. As history marched on, man wandered further and further away from any knowledge or understanding of how things were designed to operate in the Kingdom. All of Yahweh's written word is the story of His desire to restore His Kingdom to its intended order.

Jesus came as part of this story. For what purpose did he come?

> But He said to them, "I must preach the Kingdom of God to the other cities also, because for this purpose I have been sent. (Luke 4:43 NKJ)

He came to "preach" the good news. He did not preach the good news about Himself, even though that certainly is good news. His purpose was to preach the good news about the Kingdom. This was His assignment.

I have said previously that all Jesus did and said was for the purpose of restoring Kingdom authority and to show us what Kingdom operation should look like. This is true. I have also said that He did what He did in order that we might become citizens of the Kingdom and pick up where He left off. This too is true. Even this, however, is a diluted, soft version of the truth.

Why are we tempted to stop at less than the truth? Why do

we not trust people with the truth? It is knowing the Truth which will make us free. Freedom frequently comes at a price, but people have a right to be free. People have a right to truth. The choice then becomes theirs.

The truth is: Jesus did what He did in order that we might become citizens of His Kingdom and that, as citizens of the Kingdom, we might become warriors enlisted in the army of the Lord, for the purpose of advancing His Kingdom in the earth. This army is necessary because the enemy who has been operating his kingdom on the earth is not willing to just roll over and return territory to its rightful owner.

We must embrace a warring mentality if we want to see His Kingdom come and His will be done on earth as it is in heaven. We must see the world as it is. We must accept that we live in the midst of a conflict between two kingdoms. The enemy's kingdom has been defeated but refuses to surrender. The kingdom of Yahweh is victorious but its citizens have not engaged in the actions necessary to reclaim the territory.

If we are going to be part of seeing His Kingdom come and His will be done on earth, we must become a militant force in the earth. We must know who our enemy is. The enemy is not other believers. The enemy is not the government or any other world system. We must be able to identify who the enemy is and what the weapons in his arsenal are. His weapons include discouragement, exhaustion, deception, and miscommunication, among others. All of his weapons, however, have one common thread running through them. This thread, the primary weapon of the enemy, is lies. His native language is lies. He cannot speak truth.

Similarly, we must know the weapons in our arsenal. These weapons include the Name, the blood of Christ, worship in spirit and truth, the preceding word of Yahweh, the gifts of the Spirit He has given to all believers, and the fruit of the Spirit which develops as we abide in Him. Our primary tool to battle the enemy, however, is truth. The truth is the way things really are. The truth is the way Yahweh says things really are. This is why the enemy seeks so diligently to keep the truth buried.

Again, we must know who our enemy is and what his tools are. We must be able to identify his tools, especially his lies. We must know what our tools are, especially truth. The other component we must come to understand is the correct order of command. When I speak of order, I do not mean that one person is more important than the other or that one person is more valuable than the other. This concept of degree of value is one which man has created. When I speak of order of command, I am referring to assignments and responsibilities.

Yahweh created the heavens and the earth in perfect order. We should not fear order. We must have order even as there is order in all of creation. We must learn to operate as a well-oiled machine. How can an army be effective if it moves about in disarray with each man doing what he thinks is right? (Remember that rogue tire which came off of our daughter's car?) How can an army be effective if it operates with each man concerned with his own glory and reward? If an army does not follow someone who has insight into the direction to go, it will never arrive at its common objective.

We are a people called to form an army, a unified force, a

body organized to advance a cause. This army, this military force, has an assignment, the same assignment originally given in the Garden. This assignment is and has always been:

> Be fruitful and multiply; fill the earth and subdue it; have dominion over the fish of the sea, over the birds of the air, and over every living thing that moves on the earth. (Genesis 1:28 NKJ)

Consider the following in this military context. The apostle receives the command to establish Kingdom order and authority in a territory. This territory is that apostle's sphere or arena of influence and responsibility. He is given the big picture, the blueprint, concerning his assignment. The enemy occupying the territory does not willingly give up the territory. The battle ensues.

This is the point at which we, the army, have failed. We have played nice with the enemy. We have agreed to cohabitation of the territory without running the enemy out. We have conceded to be nice little Christians as long as he stays a nice little devil. We have not understood the assignment. Our assignment is not about building cozy little churches with wonderful programs that keep everyone occupied and happy. It is not about operating hospitals or nurseries. It is not even about filling the ark with as many souls as we can get in! Our assignment is about taking territory for the Kingdom and establishing Kingdom order and authority in that territory. This is the truth that is revolutionizing the ecclesia of Yahweh! An army is rising up throughout the earth. This army is embracing its assignment and coming into order.

Because of the goodness of Yahweh, great hurdles have been overcome! We are no longer afraid of order. Indeed, the people of Yahweh are crying out for order. We have come to understand that all assignments are given under the prerogative of Yahweh. We now also understand that all assignments are equally important.

What happens in conjunction with the apostle receiving the command and plan to take a territory? We see the function of the prophet rise. What does the prophet do? He sees and hears from Yahweh concerning spiritual activity in the territory. He, in essence, eavesdrops on the enemy's plans. He intercepts the enemy's communication. He detects enemy movement. He receives intelligence concerning the enemy's strengths and weaknesses in the territory. He also receives instructions from Yahweh concerning counter measures and how to carry out Yahweh's plan in the territory. The prophetic serves as the intelligence branch of the military force.

What does all of this mean for the body? It means that, as the apostolic grace is increased in you through being taught, trained, and activated, you will see the big picture for your territory, i.e., your assignment over which you have been given responsibility. In other words, you will gain the Kingdom perspective for your assignment or area of responsibility, whether it be home, job, local ecclesia, etc. It also means that as the prophetic grace is increased in your life through being taught, trained and activated, you will see and hear into the spiritual realm concerning the activity of the enemy and how to counter him in order to carry out the big picture and concerning the purposes of Yahweh in order to effectively join with Him to see His Kingdom come, His will be done, on earth as it is in Heaven.

THIS IS BEGINNING TO LOOK LIKE AN ARMY ON THE MOVE!!!

CHAPTER SEVEN
THE TEACHING GRACE

I initially assumed that I would simply move through the list of graces found in Ephesians 4:11: apostle, prophet, evangelist, pastor, teacher. As I approached my next step, however, I could not shake a nagging draw to 1 Corinthians 12:28 NKJ:

> And God has appointed these in the church: first apostles, second prophets, third teachers, after that miracles, then gifts of healings, helps, administrations, varieties of tongues.

The question that arose in me was one concerning the importance of order of assembly. In the Kingdom, restoration of proper order is critical. If Holy Spirit is nudging, I have found it wise to give close attention.

Frequently, Holy Spirit will prompt me to read a passage in reverse order. When I do this to I Corinthians 12:28, it reads like this:

God has appointed these in the church:

1. Varieties of tongues
2. Administrations
3. Helps
4. Gifts of healings
5. Miracles
   Before that
6. Teachers
   Before that
7. Prophets
   Before that
8. Apostles

First, before prophets, apostles were appointed. Next, or second, before teachers, prophets were appointed. Next, or third, before evangelist and pastors, teachers were appointed. This is the order of appointment. This is the order of assembly. Much as there is an order in assembling an engine or a dish of lasagna if you want it to turn out successfully, there is a designated order of assembly in the ecclesia if we want it to turn out successfully. Could this be part of the reason the ecclesia has not yet fulfilled her assignment?

To appoint means, "to set, to put, or to ordain." To ordain means to officially establish or place in order. This sounds important enough to me to alter the plan I had and discuss the grace of the teacher next.

The understanding of one as being a teacher has been diminished to refer to one who instructs in previously established knowledge or information. Someone other than the teacher receives the information. The teacher is only responsible to be able to regurgitate this information to those under instruction. This understanding falls far short of the example Christ gave us as the ultimate Teacher.

In Aramaic, the word translated "teacher" in I Corinthians 12:28 is *malpana*, a person of high intelligence and disciplined study, but who has done so informally outside of rabbinical schools. This is also the word used in Ephesians 4:11.

With Yeshua as our example of the greatest teacher, we see in Matthew 5:1–2 (NKJ):

> And seeing the multitudes, He went up on a mountain and when He was seated His disciples came to Him. Then He opened His mouth and taught them saying . . .

He taught them. He gave them instruction. However, He did not simply convey knowledge or information previously received and established by another man. He gave them living words of revelation concerning what Father was saying. He explained and expounded upon what He was saying and doing to demonstrate Kingdom order and authority. He taught what the Kingdom should look like and how it should operate. He taught Kingdom! He taught things they had never heard before. And, what He said got Him in trouble with the religious crowd. It is not unusual for truth to offend.

Yeshua challenged the existing and accepted "knowledge" and understanding of His day. He brought truth. He said some hard things as He repeated what Father was saying. In obedience, He was compelled to instruct truth, i.e., the way things really are. It was messy. When things are a mess, it might get messy trying to fix it. This should come as no surprise.

We see New Testament examples of teachers in Acts 13:1–14 where reference is made to certain prophets and teachers. Also, we see this in I Timothy 2:7 and II Timothy 1:11, where Paul refers to himself as a teacher. Apollos is referred to as a teacher in Acts 18:24–25. What did these teachers teach? They did not teach the Epistles. In fact, they did not teach the New Testament at all. They lived it. They did not teach the law and the prophets according to the Old Covenant. What did they teach? What would we teach if we had no New Testament? How would we know anything if we only had Old Testament scriptures? We would have to teach the way they did, by revelation, which comes out of relationship with Father. In fact, Yeshua taught His followers some things that they did not understand when being taught. It was only after they were open to revelation that they began to understand.

If they did not teach New Testament scripture and they did not teach according to Old Covenant law, what did they teach? They taught revelation of the Kingdom. They taught Old Testament scripture as it relates to Kingdom. They followed the example of Yeshua and, through relationship, received revelation of truth, the way things really are. This is what they taught.

The question is this: "How are we to know truth?" Is the answer that we should just look in the Bible? Unequivocally, no! The Bible is true but it is not ALL of the truth. Please delay my stoning until you read and consider a little further:

> I still have many things to say to you; but you cannot bear them now. However, when He, the Spirit of truth, has come, He will guide you into all truth; for He will not speak on His own authority, but whatever He hears He will speak; and He will tell you things to come. He will glorify Me, for He will take of what is Mine and declare it to you. (John 16:12–14 NKJ)

Yeshua spoke truth. Holy Spirit came and led New Testament believers into all truth and He still is:

> But, as the Tanakh says, "No eye has seen, no ear has heard and no one's heart has imagined all the things that God has prepared for those who love him." It is to us, however, that God has revealed these things. How? Through the Spirit. For the Spirit probes all things, even the profoundest depths of God. (I Corinthians 2:9–10 CJB)

Has Holy Spirit stopped speaking? He has not! He is still speaking insight into the true nature of things. He is still leading believers into all truth. We must diligently seek out truth that has been buried under lies or distorted by religion or the traditions of men. We must receive truth being released today by Holy Spirit. It is the height of arrogance for man to say he has all truth and close his hearing to the voice of Yahweh!

The interesting thing is that truth has never changed. By definition, if something is truth, it is, always has been, and always will be truth! Men might deny truth or fail to understand truth, but that makes it no less true. For example, men once believed it was truth that tomatoes are poisonous. This was never truth even though it was believed. Therefore, if truth is the way things really are, and if truth has never changed, then the way things really are has never changed.

Yeshua taught us and showed us the way things really are. He then told us that Holy Spirit would continue to lead us into the way things really are. He would lead us into all truth. We do not know all truth yet, but what do we know? We know we have an assignment to fill the earth, subdue it, and have dominion. We know there are Kingdoms of light and of darkness. We know that we, as believers, belong to the Kingdom of light whose King owns all and has all authority. We know we have the responsibility as citizen soldiers to take and occupy our assigned territory.

We have exposed the truth that we must make use of our spiritual senses in order to successfully engage in a spiritual war with a spiritual enemy. We must have these spiritual senses exercised and brought to maturity under the impartation of the grace of the prophet. We have exposed the truth that we must become Kingdom thinkers and doers. This will take place as we receive of the grace, power, and equipping for ministry of the apostle and come into Kingdom order of governance.

This being said, what is the responsibility of the teacher? Is it the responsibility of the teacher to discover truth and instruct others in that truth? That is what we have defined as the responsibility of the teacher to be. While this is something a teacher does, it is not who a teacher is. A teacher is a bringer of truth, a disperser of understanding. It is not a teacher's responsibility to find all truth and tell believers what that truth is. This is the fallacy we are moving away from.

As a bringer of truth, a teacher takes Kingdom thinking and acting and spiritual insight and communicates it in an understandable way as truth, the way things really are. This might include exposing a lie. It might challenge our comfort. It will most certainly expose religious and cultural traditions. A teacher takes spiritual revelation and translates it into Kingdom application.

Still, this is what a teacher does. We have yet to answer the question concerning what a teacher is responsible for imparting out of who he is. As with all believers, the teacher's first responsibility is to be who he was created to be. Who is a teacher created to be? As one of the five gifts of Christ, what does a teacher carry? What does a teacher carry which he is then responsible for imparting to believers in order that they might come to unity of the faith? You see, one person cannot impart to another what he does, but rather what he carries or who he is.

What is the grace that a teacher carries which makes him who he is? This grace, this power and equipping for ministry, is what he is responsible for imparting to believers. The grace he carries, the motivating drive in his life, is the desire for truth, the desire to know the way things really are. This truth cuts through tradition, culture and prior knowledge. The teacher loves truth. The teacher will not be satisfied with anything less than truth. The teacher feeds truth, carries truth, and imparts the desire for truth to believers. As believers receive this impartation of the desire for truth, they begin to seek truth, feed on truth, and feed truth to others. In this way, the grace of the teacher, the desire for truth, is multiplied in the earth.

How does the teacher work with the apostle and prophet? How do they function together to bring order and maturity into the Kingdom? The focus of the apostle and prophet is on the heavenly realm. Their attention is on the spiritual realm. The teacher works with the apostle and prophet to translate the truths of Kingdom understanding and insight received through the exercise of spiritual senses into practical application. If you will, the teacher creates a bridge of understanding between the graces that have a heavenly focus, the apostle and prophet, and the graces that have their focus and assignment more in the direction of the body, the evangelist and pastor. As the body is exposed to the grace of the teacher, we will have imparted to us a desire to seek truth. We will receive truth by exercising our spiritual senses because of the grace imparted to us by the prophet. We will see and understand how this truth operates in the Kingdom because of the grace imparted to us by the apostle. In other words, we will receive revelation of the truth, the way things really are, by exercising our spiritual senses, and we will see and understand how things really are meant to operate in the Kingdom. As a result, we will begin to live based on truth—the way things really are. His Kingdom will come. His will will be done on earth as it is in Heaven.

CHAPTER EIGHT
THE EVANGELISTIC GRACE

We all have an idea of what we think the function of an evangelist is. The function of an evangelist, as we know it to be, has been very visible in the media age. We expect that well-known evangelists should hold big crusades and less known ones should hold smaller events. Maybe they should travel. Maybe they should be missionaries. Maybe they should stand on a street corner and scream hellfire and brimstone. Maybe they should take groups of people to hand out water or food baskets or maybe they should go door-to-door handing out tracts. Regardless of their method of operation, however, certainly they are the ones responsible for getting souls saved. That is their job! Right? No. That is Holy Spirit's job.

If what we have come to accept as truth concerning the function of the evangelist is not true, what is? Ephesian 4:11 says the evangelist is responsible to teach, train, and activate believers in the evangelist grace they carry in order for believers to be administrators of the Kingdom of Yahweh on the earth as an expression of this grace.. It is the responsibility of the evangelist, as it is with the apostle, prophet, and teacher, to multiply himself in others as part of the full expression of Christ.

What does it mean when I say that the evangelist should multiply himself? First, it means that he is not to be one of a small, elite group of "called" believers out there getting people saved. Yes, their driving desire is to see people become believers, but not just to fill churches and not only to escape hell! We have told the evangelist that it is his responsibility to stir the waters for salvation among unbelievers. Ephesian 4:14, however, tells us that his assignment is to teach, train, and activate believers in the grace he carries. We have sent him out to the unbelievers when Christ gave him to believers!

The evangelist, on the other hand, like the teacher, has been skating along accepted, received, and celebrated in their traditional, well-defined roles in the church just as they are. We have believed that teachers are supposed to teach Bible stories and feed predigested information to people too lazy or unmotivated to search things out for themselves. In the same way, we have believed that evangelists are the ones who are supposed to get souls saved. These are our definitions, but when we search out truth, when we place Kingdom at the forefront, we see that there is much we must unlearn. There are lies we must discard. There is truth we must embrace even when it is uncomfortable. We must not try to force the preceding revelation of Yahweh into old understanding. Tradition and culture must be separated from truth.

The emerging evangelist is seeking to operate in his true function, in the way things really are. He is learning to hear and obey. He is learning to be strategic in his efforts. He is learning to operate in the grace, the power and equipping for ministry, that he was called to by Yahweh in order that he might complete his assignment to teach, train, and activate believers in that grace.

In the *Complete Jewish Bible,* Ephesians 4:11 refers to evangelists as "proclaimers of the Good News." In the Aramaic the word evangelist is not used but rather "preachers." In Greek, preacher is *kerux,* meaning "a herald" or one who issues forth a proclamation. In many modern translations we see the word evangelist, which comes from the Greek euangelistes, meaning a messenger of good news or a preacher of the gospel. Webster defines evangelist as someone who talks about something with great enthusiasm. So who is an evangelist, preacher, herald?

A preacher is one who issues forth a proclamation as by a herald. By definition, a herald is one who, in organized combat, has certain duties such as making announcements and rallying those engaged in the battle. This person typically has an official status such as emissary and acts as a courier between leaders. This person might be one who goes before or precedes the one he represents, making way for his arrival. He may also be one who proclaims or brings good news in full measure.

From this understanding, we conclude that Christ gave some the grace, supernatural empowerment to:

1. Bring in <u>full</u> measure the message he has been given
2. Announce with enthusiasm

3. Be a courier between leaders in war as a representative or emissary of the one he serves
4. Rally followers for battle

In rallying or marshalling followers for battle, he is responsible for not only gathering followers but also for seeing that they are arranged in proper order. All of this sounds like the evangelist is part of a military force and has a specific assignment in that force.

The evangelist of Ephesians 4:11 is assigned to bring in full measure the message of the Kingdom which he has been given. This message is not just that Christ lived, died, rose again, and if you accept Him as Lord and Savior you can go to Heaven one day. The message of the Kingdom delivered in full measure is that Christ defeated the enemy and because of Him we can now fulfill the assignment given to man in Genesis 2:28 to fill the earth, subdue it, and have dominion. But first, we, as an army, must take back territory. The evangelist is a rank and file leader. While the apostle maps the big picture and identifies assignments to accomplish the goal, the evangelist works on the rank and file level to see that there are personnel available to see these assignments implemented.

Our Example

How is the evangelist to convey the message that, as a military force, we must take territory back from the enemy in order that we might fulfill our Genesis assignment? We will consider Philip as our example. Philip was one of the seven named deacons in Acts 6. We see him again in Acts 8:

> Then Philip went down to the city of Samaria and preached Christ to them. And the multitudes with one accord heeded the things spoken by Philip, hearing and seeing the miracles which he did. For unclean spirits, crying with a loud voice, came out of many who were possessed; and many who were paralyzed and lame were healed. And there was great joy in that city. But there was a certain man called Simon, who previously practiced sorcery in the city and astonished the people of Samaria, claiming that he was someone great, to whom they all gave heed, from the least to the greatest, saying, "This man is the great power of God." And they heeded him because he had astonished them with his sorceries for a long time. But when they believed Philip as he preached the things concerning the kingdom of God and the name of Jesus Christ, both men and women were baptized. (Acts 8:5–12 NKJ)

In this, we see that he "preached Christ" to them. He proclaimed. He brought in full measure as a herald. He told it all! What was that all? The all he brought in full measure was the, "things concerning the Kingdom of God and the name of Jesus Christ." (v. 12) The people heard Philip and saw the miracles and deliverance he performed (v. 6–8). Many believed and were baptized because of what they heard and what they saw:

The Evangelistic Grace

> Now an angel of the Lord spoke to Philip, saying, "Arise and go toward the south along the road which goes down from Jerusalem to Gaza." . . . Then the Spirit said to Philip, "Go near and overtake this chariot." . . . Now when they came up out of the water, the Spirit of the Lord caught Philip away, so that the eunuch saw him no more; and he went on his way rejoicing. But Philip was found at Azotus. And passing through, he preached in all the cities till he came to Caesarea. (Acts 8:26, 29, 39–40 NKJ)

Philip received instructions from an angel and obeyed. (v. 26–27) He received further instructions through the exercise of his spiritual senses as Holy Spirit spoke to him. (v. 29) After completion of his assignment, Philip was transported through time and distance and was found about twenty miles away in Azotus (v. 39–40) and began preaching, bringing in full measure, along the way until he came to Caesarea (v. 39–40).

We encounter Philip again in his home in Caesarea:

> On the next day we who were Paul's companions departed and came to Caesarea, and entered the house of Philip the evangelist, who was one of the seven, and stayed with him. (Acts 21:8 NKJ)

We see him here identified as "one of the seven" spoken of in Acts 6:5. Here he is also referred to as an evangelist. The Aramaic translation refers to him as "Philip the Proclaimer." The *Complete Jewish Bible* refers to him as "Philip the Proclaimer of good news." Recall that a proclaimer is one who brings in full measure. He spoke and demonstrated the Kingdom and the name of Jesus. He exercised his spiritual senses in receiving instructions. He defied the laws of nature by being translated through time and space. In short, he lived the way Jesus had shown him to.

What do we learn from Philip? We learn that the message he shared was of the Kingdom (v. 12). He brought the full measure of truth concerning the Kingdom of God and Jesus. He did so in word and deed. He delivered this message wherever he went. We see him first in Samaria (v. 5), then somewhere between Jerusalem and Gaza (v. 26). We next see Philip in Azotus (v. 40). From there we see that he shared the story from Azotus in all cities until he reached Caesarea (v. 40) where it appears he made his home. In short, Philip recruited soldiers for the army of the Lord wherever he went.

We have heard it said that the evangelist has a driving passion for getting souls saved. We have for some reason translated this to mean that the evangelist is the one who is responsible for increasing church membership by getting people saved. However, this is not his responsibility as we see in Matthew 16:18 (NKJ):

> And I also say to you that you are Peter, and on this rock I will build My church, and the gates of Hades shall not prevail against it.

In fact, it is Christ who is responsible for building the church.

THE EVANGELISTIC GRACE

Not one soul will be saved because I want them to. Yeshua paid the price. Yet, not one of those given to Him by His Father will *not* be saved. He is well able to do His job. We need to let Him do His job, find out what our job is, and do it.

This might sound callous. It might sound as though value is not placed on souls being saved. This is not true! There is great value in souls being rescued from the enemy's camp in order to be part of the army that takes territory for the Kingdom. We celebrate souls being saved for purpose! We do object, however, to the salvation message alone. It is not the whole truth! The position we take is that the enemy is not greatly concerned about losing a few souls as long as he gets to keep territory. It is the responsibility of the evangelist to teach, train, and activate believers to enlist recruits for the army and rally these troops for action.

The evangelist cannot help but bring the message of the Kingdom in full measure in word and deed, in other words, to preach. However, like Philip who heard the voice of an angel and of Holy Spirit, the evangelist effectively exercises his spiritual senses and operates in signs and wonders. As he effectively delivers the Kingdom message in full measure in word and in deed, people will be rescued or "saved" from the camp of the enemy and will become part of the army of the Lord.

It is a fact that there is an enemy who once held me captive. One day I was shown the Door to my prison and I walked through it to freedom. When I walked out, I did so as part of an army whether I knew it or not. And, in fact, I did not! No one told me the truth! I walked right into a battle that was raging in a war that had already been won. But, again, I did not know anything about it. If only I had known the truth! Not only could I have been more effective as a soldier, but I might have avoided many wounds along the way. If only I had known that, as a soldier, I have an assignment. As a soldier, I have a purpose. What a difference the truth might have made. In the same way, you are a soldier. You have an assignment. You have a purpose.

Simply telling people about the wonders of salvation is doing them a great disservice! When they wake up one day in the thick of battle and realize things are not always lovely, they might well become disillusioned. They might feel bewildered to find themselves in the midst of something they did not know they were signing up for. They might become exhausted from trying to ride things out.

The proclaimer of the good news, the evangelist, tells the whole truth. It is not up to him who believes and joins the cause. His real work begins after they believe. After they believe is when he encourages them to jump in and be part of Kingdom restoration. He lets them know they are valued and in for an incredible journey in the army. He imparts zeal for the cause of Yahweh. That infectious zeal then spreads to others they come in contact with.

That zeal for being part of the army is not enough on its own, however. The troops must then have the desire for truth imparted to them under the influence of the grace of the teacher. They must have their spiritual senses awakened under the prophetic grace. They must have a Kingdom mindset imparted to them and assignments issued through the apostolic grace. In other words, the troops must be trained! With training comes increased confidence, effectiveness, and enthusiasm.

Imagine an army of believers taught, trained and activated in this way. This army we are beginning to see come into focus might have difficulty operating in much of our current church structure, which operates more as a bunker than a base camp. The church was never meant to be a place where people of like mind go to hide from those not like them for fear of being contaminated. Surely the ecclesia of Yahweh is to be strong enough to do more than just occasionally venture out only to quickly run back to the safe confines of common religious belief.

How does the fivefold evangelistic grace operate out of a base camp? At the base camp he receives insight concerning the Kingdom assignment for that base camp which Yahweh has revealed to the apostle of the territory. He works with the prophetic grace to gain spiritual insight into the means to accomplish that assignment. He works with the teaching grace to see this information effectively assimilate to the rank and file troops. He rallies these troops, imparting confidence and enthusiasm to them. These troops, as carriers of this evangelistic grace, now leave the base camp and go out to take territory. They find captives in the camp of the enemy and show them to the Door of freedom. Once free, these new recruits then are taken to the base camp for training and assignments of their own. Purpose is imparted into their lives, and, the cycle repeats. Thus, the Kingdom of Yahweh is expanded in the earth.

CHAPTER NINE
THE PASTORAL GRACE

I have discovered something during this journey. I have discovered that truth will challenge our traditions. I have also discovered that the real battleground is in my soul, i.e., my mind, emotion, and will. This is where the truth either wins or loses. The truth, however, never changes.

If I refuse truth it is my loss. I will be the one who remains in bondage. It is my life that will not be fulfilling. It is my assignment that will go uncompleted. Therefore, we must overcome the challenge and embrace truth. Now, we press on.

The position of pastor has come to be honored with almost reverential fear. In many circles we have been taught not to question the pastor. Pastors have been placed in a position of having the most power, the greatest authority, and the ultimate responsibility. This has been their position. We are not concerned with position, however, but rather with function. We count no man or his gifting to be superior to another. Nor do we count one gifting to be capable of imparting the full expression of Christ in the earth. If this means that in discussing the function of the pastor, we touch a sacred cow, so be it.

The word pastor in Ephesians 4:11 would be better translated "shepherd," A shepherd is one who nurtures a flock. One who nurtures is one who gives care and attention to someone or something that is growing or developing. To nurture means to assist in the growth, development, and success of another by providing whatever they need. The function of a shepherd is to see to the success of something or someone by facilitating what they need in order to complete their assignment. This is success: that one fulfills his assignment. It is not the job of the shepherd or pastor to gather people around his assignment in order to see it completed. Too often we have seen men gathering people to themselves who will "sell out" to their vision rather than seeking to teach, train, and activate people into their assignments. This should not be so.

Another paradox we see concerning the pastor is that many have been called pastor who are not. In our ignorance, we have required that one who leads a local gathering be called a pastor. As a result, we have many people being called pastor who were never called by Yahweh to be pastors. We have people out of place and being required to operate outside of their assignment. We have people frustrated because, in spite of having a true desire to serve Yahweh, they are being required to wear other men's shoes. We see people around them frustrated and unfulfilled because they cannot find order in a system that is out of order. The pastor, of all of the five graces, is the one most in need of stepping into the liberty of who he is created to be.

How did we get to where we are in placing pastors in the position of head of the church? It certainly did not begin this way. In the first century church we see a multiplicity of leadership in local gatherings. In Acts 13:1 we see teachers and prophets ministering together. Acts 14:23 finds elders being appointed to both teach and pastor. Whatever its appearance, we do not see the leadership of a local gathering primarily in the hands of one man.

Due to the severe persecution followers of Christ suffered in the first century, I can imagine that there might have been great relief when the Roman government under Constantine embraced believers and invited them to be part of the existing governmental system. But, at what cost? There ensued the formation of an organized church structure very reminiscent of Old Covenant order in which there was an established priestly order out of which all ministers were named. In this Old Covenant order there were buildings and properties to be maintained through the moneys of the faithful. In this system, the gatherings had an established order and all authority was in the hands of the elite priestly order. During the Reformation, the title of priest was changed to "vicar" or "pastor" but the structure remained much the same.

Today, whether it be denominational, charismatic, or evangelical, our local structure remains much the same, and foreign to what the first century church looked like when Peter spoke concerning the "priesthood of all believers" (I Peter 2:9). Even in today's "progressive" circles and "free" churches we have rigid rules of order which do not look very different from Old Testament order with one man in charge, with one or a handful of men hearing for the rest, with large volumes of money being paid for maintenance of properties, and much of this into Babylon. It is also as if when believers fell into bed with the Roman government, the Babylonian system of that day, there began a spiral back to Old Testament forms placing the position of pastor where the Old Testament priest once stood.

Do not blame the pastors! Many who have sincere desire to serve and know they are called took the title because it was the only one available for what they felt called to do. The title of evangelist was available, but only if one felt led to travel and do the acceptable evangelist "stuff." The title of teacher was available, but one called teacher was relegated to Sunday school or Bible study. Apostles and prophets were equally ill-defined, if not altogether rejected. If one did not feel called to fit into any of these equally ill-defined boxes, his only choice was to be called pastor and do pastor stuff.

Therefore, pastor or not, men tried to fit themselves into the pastoral box. If they were not created to be pastors, they would experience frustration and lack of fulfillment. In the end, those gathered with them would suffer and experience their own frustration at being stripped of their own priestly rights and responsibilities. If one was indeed created to be a pastor, he would find himself burdened with responsibilities he was never meant to carry, leading to equal frustration.

What result has this faulty structure had in the Kingdom? It has stripped believers of their priestly rights and responsibilities. It has placed them in bondage to religious order. With each new revelation came a new religious culture, which drew a group of followers to itself. This new religious culture would then multiply itself under the leadership of one man who was adequately indoctrinated in the new revelation. The survival and validation of the new culture was dependent upon its ability to get followers who would commit themselves to the new thought and its leadership. Autonomy of thought was sacrificed for the good of the culture.

In addition, the faulty structure of having a one person, positional hierarchy leadership under the pastoral grace left the church without equal expression of the five graces of Christ. With the pastoral or nurturing grace at the helm, we were left with a church focused on caregiving with occasional spurts of expressions of the other graces when other graces made appearances at local gatherings. The church became first a place of shelter and provision for the needs of its members. Buildings grew. Programs grew. Needs became many and varied. In order to keep the wheels turning, it became necessary to please people so they would stay to help keep the machine running. In this way, the church became a bunker rather than a base camp. It became a place of gathering in. In fact, seeing people made completely whole would be counterproductive to the goal of keeping people dependent upon the organization. However, no army promotes the cause of its king by staying within the walls of the fortress.

I conclude then that the function of pastor was never meant to be supreme church authority. I further conclude that none of the other four functions was ever meant to be supreme authority either, but that Christ gave apostles, prophets, teachers, evangelists, and pastors to teach, train, and activate all believers to operate in their priestly authority. The caregiving, nurturing function is vital, but it is only one part of the expression of Christ given to the church. Remember, as stated earlier, to nurture means to help to grow, develop, and succeed, to take care of someone or something that is growing or developing by providing food, shelter, protection, and so forth. It is the "to help to succeed" or accomplish their assignment that got lost in the busy work of church business.

If we remove the misconception concerning the function of the pastor as being the one person in charge and the one person responsible, what are we left with? Jesus said of Himself that He is the Good and Great Shepherd. What does a shepherd do? He watches over to protect. He makes sustenance available. He watches for injured sheep and gets them care. The shepherd desires strong sheep, which produce high quality wool, i.e., the fruit of their existence. If in a fold at night, the shepherd becomes the door to keep danger out during the times of rest. But, when rest is over, he opens the door and steps aside to send the sheep out.

What does this look like if we apply it to our Kingdom base camp analogy? What would the pastoral grace look like? How would the pastoral grace function as a shepherd or nurturer also known as a caregiver or one who gives help and protection? In keeping with our military analogy, how would this function fit in?

At a base camp there will be several operations going on simultaneously. Among these there will be an infirmary where the sick and wounded receive help to recover and gain strength. There will be a mess hall where nourishment is dispersed. There will be a commissary where supplies are available. There will be an armory from which weapons are issued. One would also find a communications center where information is received and appropriately dispersed. In addition there might be weight rooms, recreations areas, counseling centers, and so forth. Each of these represents an area that provides assistance in one way or another to the soldiers in the camp. The people in charge of giving this assistance are helpers or caregivers in one way or another. If you have need in one of these areas, you go to one of these people.

If we translate this to consider a Kingdom of warriors, what would it look like? In this context, what would the pastoral grace look like, given that he is a shepherd or nurturer? Recall that a nurturer is one who helps other to grow, develop, and succeed. He is someone who cares for someone or something who is growing or developing by providing food, shelter, protection, and whatever else they might need in order to succeed. These people could be called caregivers. At every Kingdom base camp there would be caregivers over various divisions of responsibility. There might even be caregivers for the caregivers to see that their need to succeed is made possible.

These base camp caregivers are all present to help with needs. They are there to ready soldiers to return to their assignments. Their motivation is to help others be ready to succeed at their assignments. The success of others is their success.

These caregivers are the logistical officers on the base. Logistics refers to things necessary to be done to plan and organize an activity or event that involves many people. In military science it also refers to the procurement, transport, and maintenance of military materials, facilities, and personnel. This person handles the details that keep the operation moving.

THE PASTORAL GRACE

It is obvious this is a very important function without which nothing would succeed. This is the pastoral grace in operation. It is people oriented and people focused, but for purpose—always for purpose. This is the grace, supernatural empowerment, that the pastor is assigned to impart to other believers.

Operating within his grace, the pastor brings balance to the big picture the apostle sees. He keeps the prophet from mowing everyone down. He works closely with teachers to identify areas in need of communication, explanation, and instruction in truth. He also tempers the evangelist, who sometimes forgets that people need a little rest and relaxation. He does not, however, function for the purpose of getting people to stay at the base camp! He does not find satisfaction in getting as many people as possible to hide out safely in his bunker. In all the pastor does as he functions in his assignment, it is for the purpose of imparting to all believers the grace to help others succeed in their assignment.

CHAPTER TEN
WE CAN DO THIS!

The church, the Ecclesia of Yahweh, is rising from the ashes to become the power in the earth she is supposed to be. She is coming into order. With that order comes the unity and authority necessary to accomplish the assignment given to man in Genesis 1:28 NKJ:

> Be fruitful and multiply; fill the earth and subdue it; have dominion over the fish of the sea, over the birds of the air, and over every living thing that moves on the earth.

The apostle, who acts as the base commander, has the big picture of the assignment in a territory. This territory might be a geographical territory or it might be an area of influence or responsibility. Whatever the case, it is the territory he has been assigned to by Yahweh, and, therefore, has authority to operate in.

He confirms giftings and assignments and releases personnel to function. He imparts this grace of establishing order to all believers in order that they might access this impartation as needed for their own assignment in their own territory.

The prophet is in charge of the intelligence division. He has oversight for teaching, training, and activating personnel in the exercise of their spiritual senses. The intelligence division serves to see and hear into the camp of the enemy to learn of his plans. Its members also see and hear into the plans of Yahweh for countering the plans of the enemy and advancing the cause of the Kingdom. They are the Kingdom secret service.

The teacher is a bringer of truth through revelation. He is gifted in knowing how to communicate information in an understandable way. He is adept at various forms of communication and is responsible for conveying understanding of purposes and plans up and down throughout the ranks. He acts to decipher and distribute information and instruction as needed.

The evangelist focuses on recruiting and enlisting soldiers for assignments. He does far more than just get people out of the enemy's prison. He must also inform them of the responsibilities they have as citizen soldiers. He must let them know that they have an important part to play in the cause of Yahweh.

The pastor's motivation is to provide whatever help is needed in order to see soldiers at every rank be successful at their assignment. They are the nerve center of the base camp, receiving those who come in and providing them with whatever is needed to make them ready to go back out. They are absolutely essential for the smooth operation of the base camp and its fulfillment of the territorial assignment.

No one person, other than Christ, carries the fullness of all of these graces. However, everyone who is of Christ can function in a measure of each of these graces as it is needed if they have had the graces imparted to them. In this way, Christ is multiplied in the earth.

It is the assignment of the five graces to teach, train, and activate all believers in each of the graces in order that all believers might be a full expression of Christ in the earth, as He was of His Father. By doing so, all believers are then equipped to be successful administrators of the Kingdom of Yahweh on the earth.

Thy Kingdom come,
Thy will be done,
On earth as it is in heaven!

WORKS CITED

Merriam-Webster.com. 2014. http://www.merriam-webster.com (July 18, 2014).

Vines, William, ed. *Expanded Vines Expository Dictionary of New Testament Words,* Minneapolis: Bethany House, 1984.

CPSIA information can be obtained
at www.ICGtesting.com
Printed in the USA
FFOW04n0734230316
22566FF